Facts About the Tasmanian Tiger

By Lisa Strattin

© 2016 Lisa Strattin

Revised © 2019

Facts for Kids Picture Books by Lisa Strattin

Harlequin Macaw, Vol 34

Downy Woodpecker, Vol 37

Frilled Lizard, Vol 39

Purple Finch, Vol 48

Poison Dart Frogs, Vol 50

Giant Otter, Vol 57

Hornbill, Vol 67

Dwarf Lemur, Vol 73

Giant Squirrel, Vol 76

Star Tortoise, Vol 79

Sign Up for New Release Emails Here

http://LisaStrattin.com/subscribe-here

Monthly Surprise Box

http://KidCraftsByLisa.com

Contents

INTRODUCTION

The Tasmanian tiger was not a tiger at all; tigers are mammals, but the Tasmanian tiger was a marsupial, which is a special type of mammal. Marsupials have many of the same traits as other mammals, such as fur (or hair) on their bodies and the ability to produce milk to feed their young. However, unlike other mammals, their young are born very, very early, and finish growing in a special pouch on the mother's belly.

This means that the Tasmanian tiger was more closely related to kangaroos, koalas, and the American opossum, than it was to actual tigers.

It got its name from the distinctive stripes, much like a tiger's stripes, that ran the length of the back-half of its dog-like body.

The Tasmanian tiger is believed to be extinct, though every few years someone will claim to have seen one in the wild.

CHARACTERISTICS

Not much is known about the Tasmanian tiger's behavior. Shortly after the animal was discovered and begun to be observed, its numbers dropped and it became harder and harder to find in the wild. The last confirmed sighting of the animal was in 1936, or over 80 years ago, as of this writing!

That their numbers decreased before they were studied is important because many animals, when faced with similar hardships, act differently than they would have in a more normal situation.

But what is guessed about the Tasmanian tiger is that it was nocturnal, which means it was mostly active at night. It is thought to have spent its days in woods, lying in dens in small caves or under fallen trees. At night, it would hunt in the pastures of Tasmania, where the animals it hunted fed and often slept. It was able to hop on its back legs, in a manner similar to a kangaroo, and it's believed that it used this ability in order to gain speed quickly, perhaps to escape danger or to chase prey.

It was shy and avoided people, but it did not avoid the farm animals, the sheep, cows, and goats, that European settlers brought to Tasmania, and because of the threat the animal posed to the settlers' livestock, they were hunted and killed by local farmers.

APPEARANCE

In Greek mythology, a chimera was a magical beast with a lion's head, a goat's body, and a snake's tail. Well, a Tasmanian tiger was something of a chimera, it had a head shaped like a wolf, a body like a lean, long dog, stripes like a tiger, and a rigid, kangaroo-like tail. It's believed to have had a brownish-yellow coat, though we can't be certain about the color of adults, photos and videos of it are all in black and white. Some of the animals were preserved in museums, but they were all young, and fur of young animals often changes color as they age.

LIFE STAGES

Tasmanian tigers were marsupials, which means that they were mammals that gave birth to live young, though they did it a little bit differently than most other mammals. Mammals like deer and horses have babies that are able to walk and run within hours. Other mammals, like our dogs and cats, have babies that are able to run within weeks.

Marsupial babies, though, are born very, very tiny. The kangaroo, for example, which grows to be as large as a tall, heavy man, starts its life about the size of your teacher's big toe! When it's first born, a marsupial will crawl out of its mother's womb and through its mother's fur, until it reaches a pouch on her belly. It will crawl inside this pouch, where its mother will feed it, and it will stay there until it's mature enough to fend for itself.

In the case of Tasmanian tigers, it's thought that they had between two and four cubs at a time, and that their young stayed in their mother's pouch for as long as three months.

After leaving the pouch, it's thought that young Tasmanian tigers stayed in their den, where they were protected from predators, until they were old enough to hunt. This is similar to the way that wolves, dogs, and even some cats act. But, again, we don't know for sure, we are only guessing!

LIFE SPAN

The few Tasmanian tigers that were captured and held in captivity lived for as long as nine years. In the wild, however, where they had to fight to find food and water, it's thought that they lived from between five to seven years.

SIZE

The Tasmanian tiger was shorter, but longer, than a medium sized pet dog. The body of an adult was between three and four feet long. It also had a tail that was around two feet long. At the shoulder, they were two feet tall, and they weighed as much as 70 pounds.

HABITAT

There are fossils and cave paintings of Tasmanian tigers on the Australian mainland, which is north of the island of Tasmania, all the way up to Papua New Guinea, which is a large island north of Australia.

However, in modern times, the animals only lived on Tasmania itself.

DIET

Some accounts list the Tasmanian tiger as a pursuit predator, which means that it chased its prey in the same way that wolves might. Other studies of its bones suggest that it was an ambush predator, which means that it hid and waited for its prey to get close, in the way that cats do. Still other studies, particularly of the bone of its front leg, suggest that it sometimes did both.

For a long time, it was thought that the animal hunted on smaller prey, in the same way that foxes and domesticated cats do. However, recent research into the strength of the animal's jaws suggests that it was as strong as a large wolf's. This means that it could have hunted animals larger than itself, in the same way that wolves and lions do. It is thought, then, that Tasmanian tigers hunted sometimes like a fox, alone and for smaller prey, but at other times like a wolf or lion, in packs, and for larger animals.

FRIENDS AND ENEMIES

The Tasmanian tiger's neighbors would have been animals that were native to Australia and Tasmania, the Tasmanian devil, kangaroos and wallabies, as well as pademelons, potoroos and bandicoots. Australia and Tasmania are also home to animals that people in the United States would be more familiar with, foxes and birds and snakes and porcupines.

All of these animals, though, would either have been prey or predator for the Tasmanian tiger. It was social within its own species, but, as far as we can guess, didn't make other friends easily.

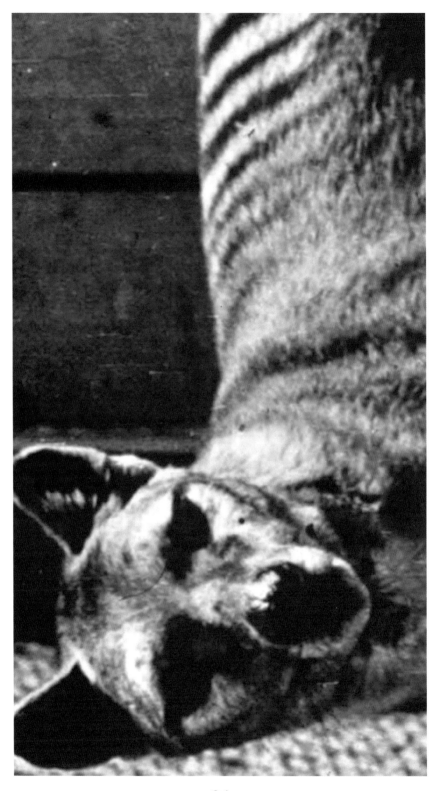

SUITABILITY AS PETS

While the Tasmanian tiger wasn't a tiger at all, it was probably just as ferocious, and was shy around people. Trying to have one of these as a pet would be like trying to keep a pet mountain lion, it might be cute when it is little, but it wouldn't be cuddly for long!

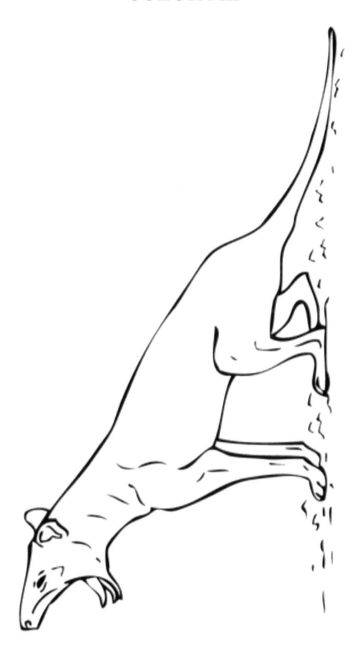

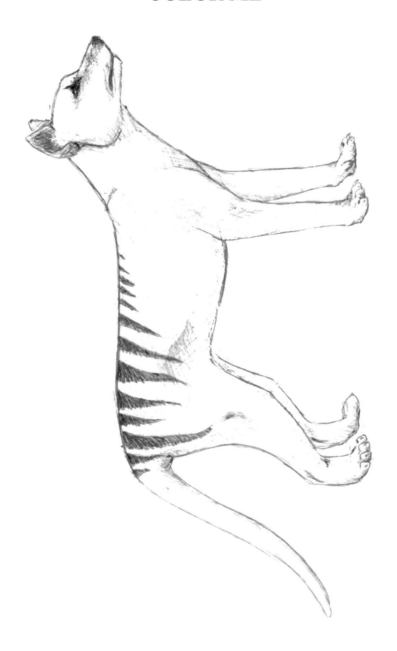

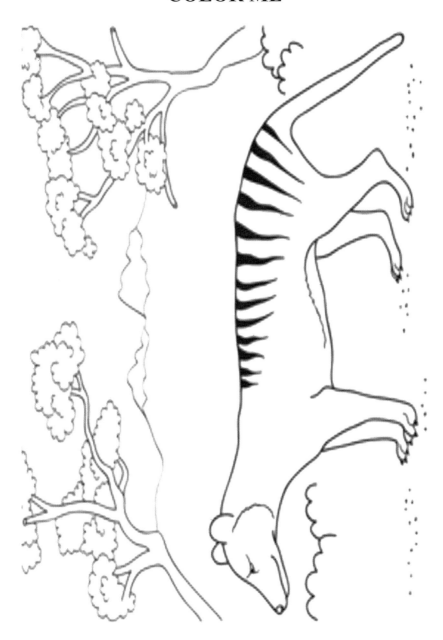

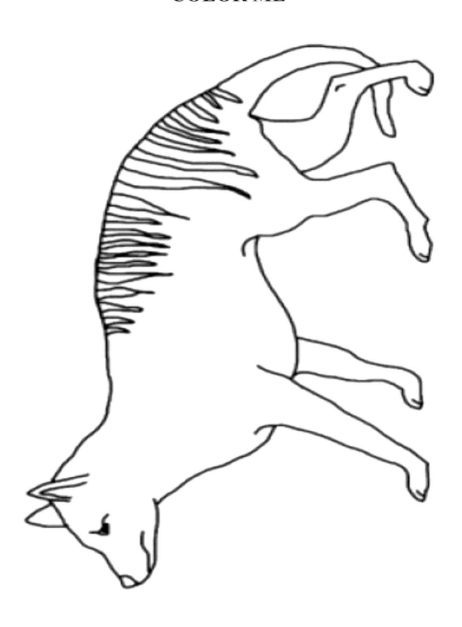

Please leave me a review here:

http://lisastrattin.com/Review-Vol-128

For more Kindle Downloads Visit Lisa Strattin Author Page on Amazon Author Central

http://amazon.com/author/lisastrattin

To see upcoming titles, visit my website at LisaStrattin.com– all books available on kindle!

http://lisastrattin.com

PLUSH TASMANIAN TIGER

You can get one by copying and pasting this link into your browser:

http://lisastrattin.com/tasmaniantiger

MONTHLY SURPRISE BOX

Get yours by copying and pasting this link into your browser

http://KidCraftsByLisa.com

Printed in Great Britain
by Amazon